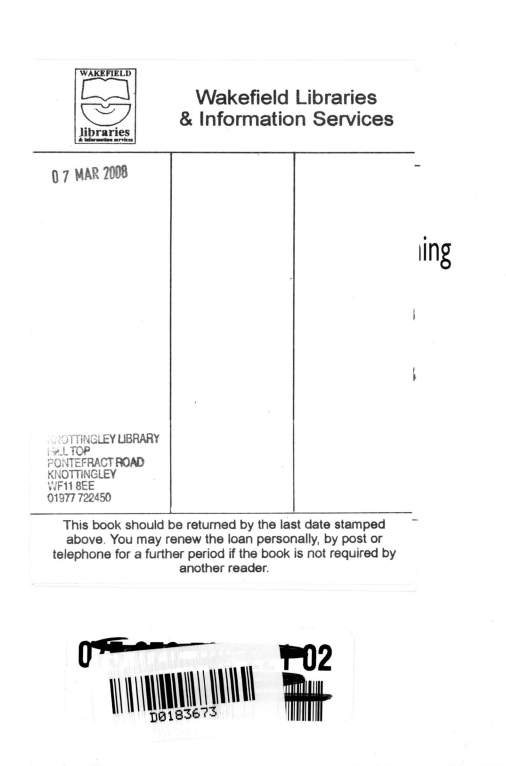

LOOKING AFRESH AT THE PRIMARY CURRICULUM SERIES

Series Editors: Kate Ashcroft and David James,
University of the West of England, Bristol

Improving teaching and learning in the humanities
Edited by Martin Ashley

Improving teaching and learning in the core curriculum
Edited by Kate Ashcroft and John Lee

Improving teaching and learning in the arts
Edited by Mary Kear and Gloria Callaway